**Adriano Cioci**

# A GUIDE TO
# ASSISI

**Edited by LITOVALD - Valdagno**
**Distributed by DACA - Assisi**

**LITOVALD**

Printed in Italy by
LITOVALD s.a.s.

Text: Adriano Cioci

**The part dedicated to the environment has been written by Antonio Giusti, officer at the Corps of Foresters.**

Graphic project: Barbara Burcini, Manuela Burcini
Edited by: Andrea Angelucci, Giovanni Angelucci, Marco Piccardi

PHOTOGRAPHIC SOURCES

Cover: Angelo Lunghi - Assisi
Back cover: Andrea Angelucci

Andrea Angelucci:
Pages:
1,3,4,5,6,7,8,9,10,11,13,14,20,21,31,42,43,44,45,48,49,50,51,52,53,56,57,59,60,61,62,63,64,65,66,67,
69,70,71,72,73,74,75,76,77,79,80,81,82,83,86,95.

Father Gerhard Ruf (O.F.M. Conv.):
Pages: 15,16,17,18,22,23,24,25,26,27,28,29,30,32,33,34,35,36,37,38,39,40,41,54,55.

Giovanni Angelucci:
Pages: 46,47,58.

Adriano Cioci:
Page: 68.

A special thanks to Father Adolfo (O.F.M. Conv.), guide of the St. Francis Basilica, for the drawing of the history of Franciscan Order.

*The charming sunsets of Assisi.*

## THE FOUR SEASONS

There are tepid evenings in autumn when the western sky fades to orange reflecting its inexplicable range of nuances on the worn out stones of Assisi. At this moment a veil of silence seems to descend on the entire valley while the sun slowly lies down beneath the silhouette of the hills of Trasimeno and then gets devoured by these - and thus the scene becomes emotion. The stones shed their red, assuming first a pink, then a violet and in the end a hue of gray . Then night falls. It is this moment of the day in which, perhaps, we best perceive the inevitable course of time. The unperceivable becomes perceivable and colour assumes the shape of the future. Assisi is a sight from this point of view as well, it is a demonstration of nature which repeats itself every day without ever getting lost in the daily routine, without becoming a slogan or dissolving its tones. Instead it lightens up the imagination and gives us space for our fantasies - thus we imagine medieval scenes with lords and ladies, women and men of the people animating this town's alleys and squares.

*The monumental complex of the Basilica di San Francesco.*

But there are cold winter evenings when the streets become deserted, the old lanterns nervously creak the north wind and the last dry leaves intrusively drag themselves along the floor. The long loud ringing of the monastery bells can be heard in alternation with the draughts and the whole scene becomes a frenetic dance which assumes the connotations of a song. Then the tolling of a bell irradiates sweet Christmas tunes anticipating silence. The wind falls all of a sudden and from the Tescio valley intermittent vapours rise.

Another spectacle is the fog on the first spring days which are still harsh, but nevertheless already perfumed with almond blossoms. From the height of the Rocca the town shows itself as if it were suspended over a snow-white ocean of cotton-wool and from time to time houses and bell towers get first devoured and then returned. Later, the sun unhinges the last bulwarks of fume and the valley pulses with a thousand colours. The swallows come back to Francis, singing. It seems as if one heard the words of the Saint: not by chance did he become a poet in this blessed land. Hence the summer softens the tones of nature and the scent of the brooms invades Mount Subasio which fills with countless voices until sunset comes and the bells announce the vespers. The sweet season is a further call to contemplation, even if the lanes converging to the centre become animated by the tourists and the bawling does not even die down at nightfall.

Four seasons to live various atmospheres in a town where history is inscribed on the walls, where it can be savoured in suggestive sights characterized by old houses with balconies brimming with flowers, a that has set the scene for indelible events, fearing not the force of centuries and withstanding the winds of time. Four atmospheres linking into one only message: the search for a past unsuccumbed by misery, a past that has created a new dimension for spirituality to manifest itself.

*Mysticism and nature: a perfect union*

*Piazza San Rufino, detail of the fountain.*

## THE HISTORY

Assisi, the capital of a new Christianity, extends itself over the western slopes of Mount Subasio like a comet of rare beauty. Its outline, a splash of colour that hesitates between pink and the red of bricks can be seen from every corner of Spoletine Valley. Its importance throughout the centuries never ceased. From the Roman period onwards, the city dominated trading, being thus a constant point of reference for this part of the territory. But its character had already been known from former periods. Beyond the legends, it seems that the place was populated by the Umbrians (Plinius explicitly referred to it), but archeological findings that give certainty have not been transmitted to us. On the other hand, there have been many important findings making possible the reconstruction of the history of the plain. Objects belonging to the Iron Age have come to light in Bastia, Santa Maria degli Angeli, Castelnuovo and Petrignano. It is certain that the mountain dominating Assisi was a place of worship for the populations of the area.

The first indications referring to an urbanization inside the city's actual periphery date back to the 6th century B.C. From this period onwards it is presumed that the centre assumed a significant role and personality, which was influenced by the Etruscan culture whose impact extended up to the gates of Assisi. In the year of 89 B.C. it became a Roman *municipium*. From this date onwards the urban structure grew more precise; monuments attributing a more distinctive characteristic to the social and cultural spirit of the city were built: boundary walls, entrance arches, funeral monuments, squares, buildings, temples, the theatre, the amphitheatre and various sculptures. Only small parts of these buildings are preserved; the ones worth mentioning are: the Minerva Temple (façade), parts of the Roman Forum, some cisterns, minor monuments and a long series of sculptures and inscriptions (most of them conserved at the Museo Romano).

After the fall of the Roman Empire, Assisi suffered the uncertainties common to most of the towns in the north and centre of Italy: in 545, after a long and bloody siege, it was subdued by the Goths, then reconquered by the Byzantines, but finally it fell into the hands of the Longobards. Thus a long period under the dominance of the Dukes of

*View of the city and the valley below*

*Winter in Assisi.*

Spoleto began. A certain cultural and political rewakening started around the year 1000 when Italy was inspired by a renewed spirit of freedom. New buildings were raised, monasteries were built or restored, the plain was reclaimed and agriculture flourished. In the 12th century it became an indipendent (Ghibelline) Commune and the fights with nearby Perugia began, but more than anything else people organized their rebellion against Barbarossa's overwhelming and oppressive power (1198). This is the climate in which Francis, the most famous citizen of Assisi, was born. In these years the power was transferred from the Duchy of Spoleto to the Church, which upheld those privileges especially ecclesiastical communities had been able obtain.

The territory of Assisi thus came under the dominion of noblemen such as Biordo Michelotti, Gian Galeazzo Visconti, the Montefeltros, Braccio Fortebraccio and Francesco Sforza. The city then returned under the rule of the Church, despite the fact that this evolution enhanced the civil fights among the different families in order to obtain the hegemony, especially between Nepis' (Upper part of town) and Fiumi's (Lower part of town).

After the tumultuous periods signed by internal power struggles and pestilences, a return under papal supremacy brought a certain tranquillity, which produced a new vitality both from a moral and a cultural paint of view.

From the 17th century onwards Assisi did not contribute anything of great importance to the historical annals, although the centuries to come did give the certainty that the city was going to have and important role to play in the life of the spirit. This conception has grown stronger during the present century, due to a number of manifestations that gave significance to some of the events that determined the course of history.

Assisi not only gave birth to St. Francis and St. Clare, the founder of the Damianites, but also to artists and men of culture who left their imprint on the path of existence through their intellectual achievements and their sensitivity: the Latin poet Sesto Properzio, the painters Tiberio d'Assisi and Dono Doni, the historians Antonio Cristofani, Francesco Pennacchi and Arnaldo Fortini.

The city, which has just under than 25,000 inhabitants today, is still enclosed by a mighty boundary wall and it conserves the typical shape of a medieval village. Inside, especially during the seventies and eighties, accomodations facilities have been increased, hotels have been renovated and made more comfortable and stores and artisan shops handing on traditional workmanship have been set up. Exhibitions and cultural events supply the tourists with support and integration meant to illustrate and remind of the past activities (especially ceramics and wrought iron as well as the agricultural products).

All in all, Assisi is a city which does not deceive, but wraps its visitors in an atmosphere of expectation and nostalgia, up to the point of enchanting and enrapturing them.

*Coats of arms and blazons enclosed in Porta San Giacomo.*

*Assisi seen from the Rocca Maggiore.*

## A LOOK AT THE CITY

A proper visit of the town needs at least three days. In this way we will not rush past the sights, but will admire them in their most hidden details. Thus we will be given the possibility to penetrate the spirit of a place that wants, first and foremost, contemplation. Only this way the great artistic treasures in it will appear to us in all their dignity. Otherwise, one ends up having only a vague remembrance of Assisi and and the most superficial of impressions.

Almost any period of the year is good for a holiday, but in the summer months there is often such a big concentration of visitors, that one could end up feeling annoyed by it. The same thing happens in late spring as well, and from Easter onwards, when a great number of German, British, American and Japanese tourists crowd the city. This is why it becomes more and more frequent to make use of November and especially during the working days when it is more likely to find the streets deserted. Furthermore, with the right weather conditions, Assisi becomes an enchantment that can be thoroughly enjoyed. This happens in January and February as well, months that guarantee tranquillity despite their climatic uncertainty. But it is also true that the these months lack religious, cultural and folkloristic events, the most important of these being dated between March and October.

Before starting the visit, it must be mentioned that a longer stay would give the possibility to undertake excursions to the old medieval fortified villages surrounding the city, thus not limiting sightseeing to just the classical destinations outside the walls. Furthermore, the tourist would have the chance to take walks along the marked path of Mount Subasio, the mountain that overlooks Assisi. This way one could get an impression of the surroundings as well and especially of the vegetation growing around the city.

In order to have a general panorama of the places we will go to, it is useful to climb the highest part of the city: the area of the Rocca

*The lanes are the soul of the town.*

Maggiore, the castle dominating the village, wherefrom a large view over the entire urbanized zone can be enjoyed.

The Rocca Maggiore can be reached by car following the ring-road with its indications. Parking is possible on the large unpaved square, then you turn your back to the monument and approach the limits of the open space. The landscape is superb: below us the old town centre spreads out, beyond it the Spoletine valley which terminates in a chain of mountains on it's southern side. In front of us, on the plain, the centre of Santa Maria degli Angeli can be clearly perceived with its big dome standing out above the built-up area. On the opposite side, there are the outposts of the Martani Mounts dotted with little villages, the shightly bigger centres of Bastia Umbra (on the right side), Ponte San Giovanni and the chief town Perugia can be seen down below as well.

From the northern extremity of the large square we start our quick route through the old centre, beginning with the monumental Basilica of San Francesco which stately rises on the Colle del Paradiso (Paradise Hill); its white front and square bell tower are characteristic. This true shrine of art and religion is visited by millions of pilgrims every year. In the background there is the Umbrian countryside which is rich with colours and cottages. We return near the main part of the Rocca and, turning around, we see the high and embattled bell tower of the Torre Civica (Civic Tower). The square below it is Piazza del Comune (Town Square), the centre of the city, whence the four main roads depart, which will guide us on our detailed visit of the monuments. Right in front of the tower there is the Church of Santa Maria Maggiore; slightly towards the East there is the dome of the Chiesa Nuova, whereas, turning our eyes more to the left, we see the façade and the bell tower of the Church of Santa Chiara, another important treasure of spirituality. Ascending again one reaches to the Cathedral of San Rufino, one of the most ancient churches in Assisi. It is easily recognizable by its gray-green dome and the bell tower that ends in a low roof. Our walk will develop around these buildings of worship.

*The Rocca Maggiore stands out above the city.*

# ROCCA MAGGIORE E ROCCA MINORE
## (Great Fort and Small Fort)

We will begin our visit with the monument behind us: the Rocca Maggiore.

Its actual structure is what has remained from the former military building which had been raised by cardinal Egidio Albornoz in the second half of the 14th century. In that period the Church built or rebuilt forts and viewing points in order to give the impression of military power. This strategy aimed at discouraging possible attacks by erecting imposing defensive structures. Arbornoz ordered the reconstruction of the Rocca of Assisi on the foundations of the existing fort, whose origin is uncertain, but which, in any case, hosted young Frederick II of Swabia until 1198. In later eras, the Rocca underwent rearrangements such as the strengthening of the donjon and the reconstruction of the dodecagonal tower placed at the northern extremity of the building. When the tension about possible wars grew weaker after the submission to the ecclesiastical power, the monument was left to its natural decline. Having been spared almost any despoilment, in recent times it flourished under restoration and it became possible to reopen it for cultural and touristic purposes. Thus these austere surroundings often host artistic exhibitions and cultural events.

The Rocca Minore (which can be seen from the Rocca Maggiore) holds a dominant position on the south-western side of the town. Once it was directly connected with the main fort by walls one could go through. From the surrounding forest several paths depart for excursions to Mount Subasio.

*The Rocca Minore among the green woods of Mount Subasio.*

## AN ITINERARY THROUGH THE TOWN

It is preferable to start a visit to Assisi in the western part of town. It contains some important monuments, first of all the Basilica of the Saint. We will start from Piazza Unità d'Italia.

The square is a strategic point for the arrival of sightseeing buses and cars. On the days of strong touristic influx it is advisable to use the parking areas outside town. From the square we climb up to Viale Marconi and, beyond Porta San Francesco, cross Piazzetta Ruggero Bonghi, then turning left along Via Frate Elia we reach the Piazzale Inferiore di San Francesco. At this point we have a wonderful perspective of the monumental structure, that consists of two churches and the monastery, built one on top of another. The arcade of the 15th century defining the four sides of the square deserves a good look. It was built to provide the pilgrims with a shelter, when they arrived in masses to honour the Saint.

Before the description of Basilica we will give a brief summary of the life of St. Francis.

# THE LIFE OF ST. FRANCIS

The chapter in history dedicated to St. Francis of Assisi will never be complete, even if the first biographers' lives are filled with details and during the centuries his thought has been widely and deeply studied. Every year the most renowned scholars, under the aegis of the International Society of Franciscan Studies, determine the state of the art, updating knowledge related to the worldly life of the Blessed Poor Man, but also casting light on the religious movements that developed from his thought. Therefore the picture can never be exhaustive. The Franciscan message was revolutionary for his age, but even now it is of great actuality for its high spiritual values. A few years ago, for example, Pope John Paul II did the seemingly impossible by uniting in Assisi religious heads from all over the world, in order to determine common aims and objectives.

Only the universal Franciscan ideals made this possible. This episode may help to understand how the figure of St. Francis is known and honoured by people of all races and religions. During the first period of his life, Francis' experiences were identical to those of his friends, full of

*The portrait of Francis by Cimabue: the most known image of the Saint (Lower Church, right wing of the transept).*

indecisions and exaltations, mistakes, and dominated by the will to enjoy himself.

He was born in the winter of 1182 from a rich family of Assisi. He was the son of the cloth merchant Pietro di Bernardone and Monna Pica. When he was born, his father was returning from one of his long trips to Provence. For this reason, although he was named Giovanni by Monna Pica, Pietro di Bernardone decided to change his name to Francesco (Francis). During his childhood countless attentions were lavished on him, especially by his mother, as if Monna Pica knew that destiny reserved great things for her son. Francis studied Latin, Provençal, Vulgar, Math (his father wanted his son to become an accountant in order to help him in his activity), music, singing. Thus he passed his youth studying, working at his father's shop and frequenting the "merry gangs" of young men that passed the nights rioting.

He was also proclaimed the king of banquets and dances because of his lively attitude toward feasts and dancing. But this happy go lucky lifestyle did not exclude unpleasant episodes of intolerance that were in contrast with the severe education given to the young man by his parents. He had a generous nature and when a beggar came to his draper's shop to beg for alms, first Francis drove him away, but then went after the poor man to ask forgiveness and to give him a bag full of coins.

When Assisi declared war against Perugia Francis was one of the first to enlist, but his dream to become a knight ended very soon, because he was taken prisoner. Francis spent a year in jail and, although he was home-sick, continued to spread courage and good humour among his companions. After his return to Assisi he became seriously ill and during convalescence he had the possibility to think and meditate about his life.

However, his dream of military glory had not yet subsided; he thus joined some companions leaving for a military campaign, but during the night, near Spoleto, the voice of the Lord made him decide to turn back. In Assisi Francis felt the unsurpressable need to give away his possessions to the poor, much to the disapproval of his father.

When he encountered a leper, instead of running away from him, he went up to him and kissed him. The episode is to be considered an important stage towards his imminent conversion.

His strange behaviour astonished the inhabitants of Assisi but, above all, his father Pietro di Bernardone, who did not want to believe that his son had changed so much and that he had so "miserably" lost him.

Francis passed his days in the surroundings of Assisi meditating by himself. Not far from the city walls there was the little church of St. Damian, a building in ruins. A voice from a Crucifix spoke to him: "Go

◄ *The Crucifix of St. Damian exhorts Francis to repair the church (Giotto, Upper Church).*

*The preaching to the birds (Maestro di San Francesco, Lower Church).*

and repair my house which has fallen into ruin". Those words remained with him for the rest of his life. The real meaning was not limited to the falling walls of the little church, but Francis began to restore San Damiano.

He sold some draperies and with the proceeds bought the material for the restoration. His father was enraged when he discovered the "theft" and, hoping "to recover" his son, led him before the Bishop. Having to choose between the renunciation of worldly goods and a return to his previous way of life, Francis chose renunciation. This was the only way he could take a decisive step towards conversion.

Francis had given a turn to his existence. Meanwhile, the news of his deeds passed the city boundaries. In the surroundings of Gubbio people went on talking about a penitent wearing a hermit's robe who had been able to tame a wolf that had spread fear and death. However, St. Francis' early followers, Bernardo da Quintavalle, Pietro Cattani, Egidio and Filippo, were from Assisi. The Porziuncola, a little church that was three kilometres away from Assisi in a wood at the foot of the hill, was the first refuge for Francis and his new companions. At Rivotorto he wrote the Rule defining their programs and in 1209 the religious order of Friars Minor was born, orally authorized by Innocent III, after he had dreamt that the Lateran Basilica was about to collapse and that a poor little man, St. Francis, had supported it. During those years Clare of Assisi met Francis several times and at last decided to follow his example. She renounced all worldly goods and founded the Order of the Poor Ladies.

The future would hold countless extraordinary events generated from the preachings of Francis and his followers.

In the meantime, the Count Orlando di Chiusi donated the Mount La Verna and in 1226 the Franciscan movement obtained from Pope Honorious III the acknowledgment of the Indulgence of the Porziuncola, the most important one for Christianity, after that of the Holy Land. After an endeavour to reach Marocco had ended in Spain (while the Friars Minor extended their preaching all over Europe), Francis landed at Acri and Damietta (1219) at the court of the Sultan Melek el Kamel and then went to Palestine. But since those long journeys had weakened his constitution, Francis decided to devote himself to preaching in places nearer to Assisi. At Fonte Colombo, near Rieti, he drew up the new Rule which was definitively approved by Pope Honorious III.

At Greccio, he prepared a Nativity Scene in memory of the Birth of Christ, giving rise to one of the most beautiful Christian traditions.

In 1224, on Mount La Verna, he received the divine reward of the Holy Stigmata. By then Francis was no longer bodily present among the people. Exhausted by privation and penance, he was entrusted to the care of St. Clare and her Sisters at San Damiano. Here he composed the Canticle of the Creatures, a highly lyrical work, in which Franciscan ideals emerge in their full strength and beauty.

At death's door Francis expressed the desire to return to the Porziuncola and here he died on October 3rd, 1226. After two years Pope Gregory IX canonized him. This was not end of St. Francis' presence in the world. On the contrary - from this moment the Franciscan message became ever stronger through the ages.

*St. Francis holds up the Church (Giotto, Upper Church).*

# BASILICA DI SAN FRANCESCO
## (St. Francis' Basilica)

Soon after the saint's death, his body was carried to the little church of San Giorgio, within the walls of Assisi. He was set there awaiting the construction of a magnificent temple where the Saint would be venerated by the believers. St. Francis had given instructions that his followers should bury him in a vast tract of land known as the Colle dell'Inferno (Hell's Hill) that was located north-west of Assisi.

The place was once used for executions, it was bleak and barren, and aroused fear and suspicion with whoever came near it. That was the reason for its name. And yet this is where one of the most impressive churches was going to be built. Thus, after the construction of the church, it became the Paradise Hill.

On July 16th, 1228, Francis was solemnly canonized by Gregory IX. The following day, the Pope laid the first stone of the Basilica.

The idea of a building that should join the ideals of poverty preached by the Saint with the need for space that could give hospitality to large crowds of pilgrims was translated by Brother Elia into a plan that aroused many controversies among the Friars of the Order.

Some of them wished to follow the thought of the Order's founder and build the church in a sober and austere style without decoration, while others saw in the construction the visible proof of the greatness of the Franciscan message.

*Perspective of the Upper Church façade and side.*

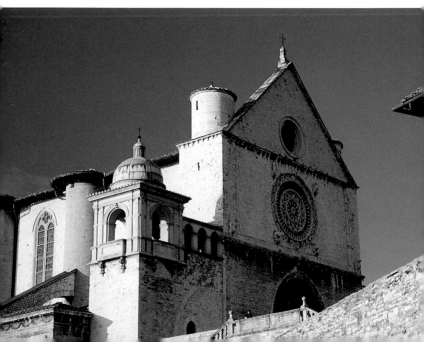

*Born from the earth, it stands out against the sky: this is the inner meaning of the Basilica di San Francesco.*

According to Brother Elia, a Tau-shaped church with two storeys expressed that message very well. In only two years, thanks to several bequests and contributions by rich believers, the lower Church was completed. There, on May 25th, 1230, the remains of St. Francis were buried.

On October 4th 1235, the building, not yet completed, received a first consecration. In 1253 Innocent IV solemnly consecrated the Basilica. By that time the structure of the temple was finished; meanwhile also the Gregorianum was built, to form a unique complex with the Basilica. It served to house the community of friars.

In order to support the construction, twelve side turrets were erected. Whereas the Upper Church was never changed, in the lower one some side chapels were built at the end of the 13th century. The walls of the Basilica were decorated with works and frescoe cycles by great Italian Masters. Among the most famous artists working in Assisi in this period, are Cimabue, Giotto, Simone Martini, Pietro Lorenzetti and others.

The history of the place did not bring substantial changes, at least until the second half of the 13th century, when the Basilica was proclaimed patriarchal, such as the Vatican, Lateran, San Paolo, S. Maria Maggiore and S. Lorenzo were. After several decades the temple was put to sack by French troops. In 1818 a first recognition of the remains of the Saint was performed (the last one was carried out in 1978). In 1939 St. Francis was proclaimed patron Saint of Italy.

*The high altar, Lower Church.*

# LOWER CHURCH

The entrance of the Lower Church is situated in the homonymous square. A Renaissance arch supported by two columns rises above a wonderful Gothic portal with two openings bordered by charming small columns  that delimit also the valuable rose window, which can be considered a fine work of art. The writing: INDULGENZA PLENARIA QUOTIDIANA PERPETUA is a consolation for the traveller who is about to enter. The shutters of the Renaissance doors are carved with scenes from the lives of St. Francis, St. Clare, St. Ludwig and St. Anthony of Padue.

## ENTRANCE AND NAVE

The entrance is not wide, but almost cosy, and this feeling is enhanced by the faint light in the interior and by the low ceilings.

On the left is the **Cappella di San Sebastiano** (Chapel of St. Sebastian), while on the right, in turn, we can see the **Sepolcro della Famiglia Cerchi**, a sepulchral monument of the 14th century dedicated to the Cerchi family, the **Tribuna** (Tribune) erected in the 15th century for the Nepis family, nobles of Assisi, the **Sepolcro dedicato a John di Brienne** (Sepulchral Monument dedicated to John of Brienne) and the

**Cappella di Sant'Antonio Abate** (Chapel of St. Anthony), now turned into a Sacramental Chapel.

At the end of the entrance transept we find the **Cappella di Santa Caterina** (Chapel of St. Caterine), done by Matteo Gattapone of Gubbio. The stained glass by Andrea di Bologna and some frescoes by Pace di Bartolo are interesting and noteworthy.

Leaving the entrance transept, we move toward the nave. The harmony of the cross vaults is enhanced by the sky blue colour, by the arches and by the wall decorations (mostly destroyed due to the opening of the side chapels) attributed to the Maestro di San Francesco. On the two sides of the nave several noteworthy chapels were built. The first on the left is the **Cappella di San Martino di Tours** (Chapel of St. Martin). No doubt it is the most interesting as far themes and quality of paintings are concerned. The chapel, indeed, was frescoed by Simone Martini who represented scenes from the life of St. Martin (the Saint divides his cloak with a poor man, he is knighted by the Emperor, Christ appears to him). The stained glass of the windows giving light to the chapel are attributed to Giovanni Bonino (1330).

We pass by the stairs descending into the saint's tomb (where we will go after the visit to the side chapels) and, still on the left, we find the **Cappella di San Pietro d'Alcantara** (Chapel of St. Peter of Alcantara), known also as the Cappella dell'Immacolata (Chapel of the Virgin) and

*The precious cross vault in the Lower Church transept.*

*Silence and suggestiveness: the Tomb of the Saint.*

from here, passing through a gate, we reach the **Tribuna di San Stanislao** (Platform of St. Stanislaw). On the right of the nave, opposite the platform of St. Stanislave we enter the **Cappella della Maddalena** (Chapel of St. Mary Magdalen).

In the frescoes of this chapel the hand of Giotto is instantly visible; the Tuscan artist painted the best known episodes from the saint's life. The scenes representing the *Unction of the feet*, the *Raising of Lazarus* and the *Noli me tangere*, where Mary Magdalen leans towards Christ, are remarkable for pictorial style and choice of colours. The next chapel is the **Cappella di Sant'Antonio da Padova** (Chapel of St. Anthony of Padua), with frescoes painted by Cesare Sermei, and at the end there is the **Cappella of Santo Stefano** e **San Ludovico d'Angiò** (Chapel of St. Stephen and St. Ludwig, king of France), frescoed by Dono Doni with masterly skill, above all in the episodes from St. Stephen's life representing the *Debate with the Jews*, the *Stoning* and the *Martyrdom*. The stained glass of the window was made by Giovanni Bonino.

# TOMBA DI SAN FRANCESCO
## (Tomb of St. Francis)

Half way along the nave a double staircase leads down to the crypt; on the right of the landing there is a niche where the remains of the Roman noblewoman Blessed Jacope de' Settesoli are buried. Opposite, several steps give access to the crypt, built in 1820, two years after the discovery of the Saint's body. It was built by the architects Belli and Brizi, but its neo classic style was completely out of tone with the sobriety of the upper churches. In 1932, Ugo Tarchi restored the area giving a more sober appearance to the crypt, thus harmonizing it with the Franciscan message. The central stone pilaster, surrounded by an iron grate is the clearest expression of the purity of St. Francis. His body is buried there, under a stone lid and all it seems to ask is silence and meditation. In the niches at the corners of the crypt are the remains of Rufino, Angelo, Masseo and Leone, four of the most devoted companions of St. Francis. In the crypt we find also the votive lamp burning with oil that is offered every year, on October 4th, in turn by the different Communes of Italy.

*St. Martin divides his cloak with a poor man (Simone Martini, Cappella di San Martino, Lower Church).*

# TRANSEPT

At the end of the visit to the Saint's tomb we come back up the stairs into the Lower Church and walk along the nave to the transept, the most interesting section in this part of the building. Above the high altar the frescoed vaults, the famous "vele" (sails) are silhouetted. They were painted by an anonymous but skilled follower of Giotto. On the cross vaults, the Master of the "vele" painted the three pillars of Franciscan thought, here called *Allegories*, because of the sense of movement and the suggestiveness the artist has conveyed upon the scenes. The sections are in turn the *Allegory of Poverty*, the *Allegory of Obedience* and the *Allegory of Chastity* and the fourth scene is the *Glory of St. Francis*. The section facing the nave is the Allegory of Poverty, representing a woman on the top of a rock spiked with brambles. Christ Himself is present and witness to the marriage of St. Francis and Madonna Poverty. Two groups of angels watch the scene, while other figures are throwing stones and beating the brambles with sticks.

In the sail toward the left transept is the **Allegory of Obedience.** Within an arcade a winged figure is seated on a throne and a friar is humbly kneeling before her. Humility is on the right and Prudence on the left. Haughtiness, symbolized by a Centaur set on the right of the arcade, is

*The Raising of Lazarus (School of Giotto, Cappella della Maddalena).*

*The Flight to Egypt (Giotto, right wing of the transept, Lower Church).*

holding back. Above the roof of the construction on the left St. Francis is standing between two angels and offers his arms to three figures (Brother Giovanni da Muro, St. Clare and Dante Alighieri), while on the opposite side, there is Penitence, a hooded figure pushing sinners in to the Abyss.

In the last allegory, the **Glory of St. Francis**, the Saint is sitting on a throne surrounded by a crowd of angels.

## RIGHT WING OF THE TRANSEPT

This section is decorated with episodes from the childhood of Christ. The paintings are attributed to a disciple of Giotto, because of their strong emotive charge. On the right of the vault (from the top downwards) the following scenes are represented: *The visitation of Virgin Mary to St. Elizabeth, The Nativity, The Adoration of the Magi, Presentation of Jesus at the Temple, Crucifixion* (with St. Francis at the foot of the cross). On the right wall is the *Madonna in Maestà with Holy Child*, frescoed by Cimabue.

Nearby is the portrait of *St. Francis* considered a reliable image of the Saint according the description given by Tommaso da Celano. On the left of the wall (from the top) there are: *The Flight to Egypt, The Slaughter of the Innocents, Jesus debating in the Temple, The Return of Holy Family to Nazareth*. Still in the left wing of the transept we can see some scenes from the life of St. Francis and the figures of five Saints

*The Crucifixion (Giotto, right wing of the transept, Lower Church).*

painted by Simone Martini (St. Francis, St. Ludwig, St. Elizabeth, the last two are perhaps St. Clare and St. Elzeario). In the adjoining **Cappella di San Nicola di Bari** (Chapel of St. Nicholas of Bari) we find frescoes attributed to Giotto's disciples containing stories about S. Nicholas. From this wing of the transept it is possible to have access to the **Cappella delle Reliquie di San Francesco** (Chapel of St. Francis Relics) where the Saint's personal belongings and records of the Franciscan movement are displayed.

## LEFT WING OF THE TRANSEPT

After having admired the valuable marble altar sustained by twenty small columns (one fluted small column contains a rib of St. John the Baptist) and having seen the frescoes of the apse vault painted by Sermei and the semicircular wooden **choir** carved and inlaid by Petrocchi (15th century), we proceed to the left wing of the transept.

The frescoes of the vault by Pietro e Ambrogio Lorenzetti are episodes from Christ's life.

From the right we have: *Jesus' entrance to Jerusalem*, the *Last Supper*, *Jesus washing the disciples' feet*, the *Garden of Gethsemani*, *St. Francis receiving the stigmata* (the Saint is represented here for his analogy with Christ), the *Crucifixion*. On the wall other scenes are connected with those previously described, but the most dramatic is the *Deposition from the cross*. Below is a *Madonna and Child*, known as the *Sunset Madonna* because it gets the best light at sunset. On this side of the transept there is the Cappella of San Giovanni Battista (Chapel of St. John the Baptist).

*Madonna and Child, known as the Sunset Madonna (Lorenzetti, left wing of the transept, Lower Church).*

*The Crucifixion (Lorenzetti, left wing of the transept, Lower Church).*

*The Resurrection (Lorenzetti, left wing of the transept, Lower Church).*

# UPPER CHURCH

In front of an ever-green lawn, that has been the theatre of religious meetings among patriarches from all over the world, we can see the magnificent façade of the Upper Church. It is built with white stone in Gothic style and can be divided into three sections.

In the lower part the beautiful portal deserves particular attention. In style and elegance it takes it's inspiration from that of the Lower Church. It is constituted by two slender columns, a pointed arch linking the two entrances and a plain rose window. The large rose window stands out in the middle section, with four skilfully decorated concentric circles. The symbols of the four Evangelists form the vertexes of an hypothetical quadrilateral. In the triangular tympanum of the upper part a round window gives balance to the structure. The small loggia to the left is a 17th century addition.

The interior of the church has a Latin cross plan and with its wonderful harmony of lights, colours and pictorial art, is religions architecture at its very best. The Italian Gothic style makes the structure slender and at the same time creates harmony in the colours. The church is a single nave, divided into four cross vaulted bays which are sustained by slender pillars. Through the mullioned windows, made precious by stained glass, golden light filters into the interior. The walls are frescoed throughout.

*The façade of the Upper Church seen from the lawn.*

The upper cycle of paintings tells Old and New Testaments stories and art historians are still discussing about their author. No doubt, on the contrary, about the painter who frescoed the lower part of the church: here Giotto and his assistants were at work. The artist painted scenes from the life of St. Francis on the basis of St. Bonaventura's account. He accurately followed the text, but his innovative pictorical technique and his poetic vision gave the 28 scenes the status of masterpieces all over the world.

The visit starts with the frescoes on the right wall of the bay nearest the transept:

1) *St. Francis is honoured by a Simple man.* In the square of Assisi with the Temple of Minerva in the background, a man bows down and spreads his cloak on the ground before St. Francis, rendering honour to the Saint's charity and humility and affirming that Francis is worthy of every respect for he is about to accomplish great things.

2) *St. Francis gives his cloak to a poor man.* On the top left of the fresco, city walls and towers can be seen. Francis meets an impoverished knight became and gives him his mantle.

3) *Francis dreams of a palace filled with arms.* During the night the Saint dreams that Christ shows him a beautiful palace. The arms in the building are meant for the Spirit's symbolic battles.

◀ *The brightness of the nave in the Upper Church.*

*The kiss of Judas, detail (School of Giotto, nave, Upper Church).*

*Francis renounces all earthly goods (Giotto, painting 5, nave, Upper Church).*

4) *Francis prays before the Crucifix of St. Damian.* During his early visit to the surroundings of Assisi, the Saint discovers a little church fallen in ruins: San Damiano. Here he prays before the Crucifix and a voice from the cross exhorts him to repair the house of God.

5) *The Renouncement of earthly goods.* The episode is a fundamental step for the Saint's conversion. Now his choice is definitive and irrevocable. The Bishop of Assisi covers him with his own mantle, while his father Pietro di Bernardone is incredulously watching the scene.

6) *The Dream of Innocent III.* The Pope sees in a dream that the Lateran Basilica is about to fall under the push of forces contrary to the Church.

And poor Francis, dressed with a frock, holds up it with his shoulder.

7) *The Rule of the Minor Friars receives oral approbation.* Francis and his early followers go to Rome to submit their Rule to Innocent III. The Pope, stricken by the friars' humility, gives his approbation to the new Order.

8) *The chariot of fire.* While the friars are asleep or at prayer in the hovel in Rivotorto, they see Francis flying in the sky on a two-wheeled Roman chariot drawn horses.

9) *An heavenly throne reserved for Francis.* A friar rapt in ecstasy sees many thrones in heaven. An angel points out to him the seat lost by Lucifer and now reserved for Francis.

10) *The devils are cast out of Arezzo.* Brother Silvestro, sent by Francis,

*Water springs from rock (Giotto, painting 14, nave, Upper Church).*

*The preaching to the birds (Giotto, painting 15, nave, Upper Church).*

goes outside the walls of Arezzo and blesses the town thus casting out the demons infesting it.

11) *St. Francis before the Sultan.* Before the Sultan of Egypt Melek-el-Kamel, Francis walks over glowing embers to prove his faith. The Muslim priests draw back afraid and refuse to imitate him.

12) *The ecstasy of St. Francis.* This is one the most idyllic scenes in the cycle. The Saint, enveloped in a bright cloud, rises above the ground towards God. The friars are amazed.

13) *The Nativity Scene at Greccio.* In a village near Rieti Francis prepares a Crib, instituting one of the most beautiful and touching Christian traditions. The Saint places a child in a manger in memory of the Birth of Christ.

14) *The miracle of the spring.* A poor man travelling with the friars is very thirsty. St. Francis prays and points to a rock from which water springs forth.

15) *The preaching to the birds.* This is one of the most known episodes in the Franciscan Legend. In the surrounding of Bevagna St. Francis preaches to the birds and they listen to his words in amazement.

*The Saint receives the Stigmata (Giotto, painting 19, nave, Upper Church).*

*Francis' death and rising to heaven (Giotto ?, painting 20, nave, Upper Church).*

16) *The death of the knight of Celano.* Francis is invited to the table of a knight of Celano, in Abruzzo. Before the end of the dinner the Saint reveals to the knight that he will die and the man falls to the ground.

17) *St. Francis before Pope Honorius III.* The scene is based on the blatant contrast between the luxury of the papal hall and the Franciscan sobriety. The Saint speaks to the bystanders and the Pope listens thoughtfully to him.

18) *St. Francis appears at the Arles Chapter.* During the Arles Chapter held by the Franciscan Order in the French town, Francis appears to one of the friars.

19) *Francis receives the Stigmata.* The episode of the Saint receiving the Stigmata on Mount La Verna is one of the most famous of the Franciscan cycle.

20) *The death of St. Francis.* The friars cry for the death of Francis surrounded by a multitude of priests. In the upper half of the scene a group of angels leads the Saint to heaven.

21) *Agostino and the Bishop* Brother Agostino is near death and wants to follow his holy father. On the right of the scene the Bishop of Assisi sees the apparition of St. Francis who tells him he is going to die.

22) *The confirmation of the Stigmata.* The knight Girolamo does not believe that the wounds in the body of Francis are real, so he comes close and touches them.

*Isaac pushes back Esau (School of Giotto, nave, Upper Church).*

*The great Crucifixion, detail (Cimabue, left transept, Upper Church).*

23) *The farewell of the nuns of St. Clare.* During the transportation of the holy body from the Porziuncola to the church of San Giorgio, the funeral train stops at San Damiano for the farewell of the nuns of St. Clare.

24) *Canonization of St. Francis.* On July 16th, 1228, in the Piazza del Comune, Pope Gregory IX canonizes Francis.

25) *The apparition to Gregory IX.* The Pope is dubious about the wound at St. Francis' side, but in a dream the Saint shows him the blood gushing forth from it.

26) *The healing of John.* A devoted follower of Francis has been assailed and wounded. He sees the Saint in an apparition and is completely healed.

27) *The woman brought back to life.* Francis implores God to bring a woman back to life. She wakes up and confesses her sins.

28) *The liberation of Peter.* A man lies in prison for a crime he never

committed. Peter implores St. Francis to set him free and immediately the gates of the prison open.

With the description of the twenty-eight panels about the life of St. Francis completed, we arrive to the left wing of the transept where we find some frescoes are attributed to Cimabue. These paintings are seriously damaged, because of the oxidization of the white lead used by the artist. In the famous *Crucifixion* we also see St. Francis falling to his knees at the foot of the cross. The other scenes frescoed in the transept depict scenes from to the Apocalypse.

In the apse, decorated by Cimabue, the precious **wooden choir** executed by Domenico Indovini in the 15th century is noteworthy. The stained glass mullioned windows of the 13th century deserve special attention, too. Then we arrive in the right transept where Cimabue painted some episodes of St. Peter's life.

At the end of the visit to the church the visitor is advised to go through the door in the transept down to the **Sacro Convento** (Holy Convent), where it is possible to observe the majestic square **bell tower**, the big arcade (that can be seen from the exterior), the Chapter Room and the Papal Room, the **cloister of Sixtus V**, the **Museum of the church** (housing important collections of sacred vestments, paintings, sculptures and various items in gold), the **Perkins Collection** and the **Library**, with the Ancient Section containing the most important documents relating to the Franciscan movement from the 12th to the 16th century.

*Archangel Gabriel (Wooden choir, Upper Church).*

*The Church of Santo Stefano (12th century).*

# TOWARDS THE CENTRE OF THE CITY

No doubt Assisi's most valuable treasure is the Basilica di San Francesco, but the town is for the visitor an inexhaustible reservoir of works of art both religious and wordly in kind. During his stay in Assisi, the medieval city structure will not remain unnoticed by the tourist, with its narrow alleys, short streets and winding lanes that are the very soul of this Umbrian town.

By proceeding along Via San Francesco, Via Arnaldo Fortini (formerly Via del Seminario) and Via Portica, one can reach Piazza del Comune (Town Hall Square), the main square of the city, where the seat of the City Government is to be found and where the administrative activities are carried out. The route is very charming and interesting.

Almost at the beginning of Via San Francesco, on the right, one can see the **Chiesina dei Cappuccini** (Little Church of Capucin Friars) and the **Museo degli Indios dell'Amazzonia** (Museum of the Amazon Indians) (at No. 19/d), a region where the Franciscan missionaries have been active for a long time. Going forward, to the left, there is a civil construction (built in the 13th century) known as the **Casa dei Maestri**

**Comacini** (House of the Masters of Como), a guild that very often worked in medieval Assisi. From this point the tourist is advised to follow the sign leading, through Vicolo Sant'Andrea, to the **Chiesetta di San Giacomo de murorupto** (Little Church of St. James of the broken wall) (at No. 18, Via Metastasio, added to the convent of the Figlie di Sant'Anna). The church (11th century) is built in a sober and bare Romanesque style and is situated in a charming and evocative setting.

Going backwards one returns to Via San Francesco. Up, to the left, are the Biblioteca Comunale (City Library) housed in the rooms of the Palazzo Giacobelli (at No. 12/f), the **Oratorio dei Pellegrini** (Pilgrim's Oratory), datable about half way through the 15th century (decorated with a great number of frescoes); the **Portico del Monte Frumentario** (Arcade of the Grain Guild) recognizable by a porch with seven arches; the **Fonte Oliviera**, built in 1570.

Beyond the arch begins Via Arnaldo Fortini (a twentieth century writer and historian). A second digression will lead the visitor to the interesting **Chiesetta di Santo Stefano** (Little church of St. Stephan), built in the 12th century. The interior is sober and striking for its bare simplicity. Frescoe fragments on the walls and the little apse deserve particular attention. According to tradition, the little bell in the tower is said to have rung at St. Francis' approaching death. Going back through Via Portica one arrives at the **Museo Civico** (Municipal Museum). The entrance hall is what remains of the crypt of the ancient church of San Nicolò, many times restructured in the course of centuries. The Museo Civico is contains a large number of tombstones, inscriptions, shafts of columns, remains of Roman statues; a narrow corridor leads to the basement of a pagan temple in the area of the ancient Forum of the Roman Municipality, below the present Piazza del Comune.

*Examples of measures (City Hall Tower, Piazza del Comune).*

*Piazza del Comune, the centre of the city.*

# PIAZZA DEL COMUNE
## (Town Hall Square)

The square has for centuries been the centre of the city's life and is so still today. Piazza del Comune has provided the scene for several episodes of Assisi's history. It forms a rectangle with a slight inclination and is surrounded by a large number of historical monuments. The **Palazzo del Capitano del Popolo**, built in 1282, was the residence of the Captain of the People, then of the Podestà. It has three storeys ending with an elegant Guelf battlement. Today it is the seat of the International Society of Franciscan Studies, important reference point for researchers in this field. On the right is the **Torre del Popolo** (People's Tower) of the 13th century. It has a quadrangular base; at the top there is the Campana delle Laudi (Bell of Praises) which has The Canticle of the Creatures engraved on it. It was given to Assisi in 1926 by the

Communes of Italy. Still on the right is the **Tempio di Minerva** (Temple of Minerva) of the 1st century. The façade is constituted by a row of six fluted columns with Corinthian capitals. The temple was transformed into the church of Santa Maria sopra Minerva. Opposite is the **Palazzo dei Priori** (Priors' Palace), the seat of the city government. It was built in three different epochs and the most ancient part is on the left hand side (13th century). Now it houses the **Pinacoteca comunale** (Municipal Picture Gallery) containing paintings, frescoes, coats of arms and decorations. Some works belong to the school of Giotto and others have been painted by talented local artists such as the Maestro Assisiate and Puccio Capanna, Andrea and Tiberio d'Assisi. The **Fountain**, on the upper half of the square, was built in 1762. The arch, on the left of the Pinacoteca's entrance, leads to the **Mostra delle Arti e dei Mestieri dell'Umbria** (Exhibition of Arts and Crafts), where some of the most significant handicrafts are displayed.

*Piazza del Comune, The temple of Minerva.*

*The Chiesa Nuova, with its elegant dome.*

## CHIESA NUOVA
**(New Church)**

From the Arts and Crafts Exhibition, we move to Piazza della Chiesa Nuova, where the homonymous church was built in 1615 according to the will of the king of Spain Philip III. The Renaissance building, in the form of a Greek cross, is vaulted by a beautiful dome. The church is interesting because it was built on the site of St. Francis' paternal home (a modern sculpture representing the parents of St. Francis is placed in the square in front of the church). Inside is the store where Francis often helped his father, the cell where Pietro di Bernardone is said to have shut his son for having sold his cloth in order to buy the material necessary for the restoration of the church of San Damiano. It is a place full of emotions and spirituality. The adjoining Monastery houses a museum (where sacred objects, pieces of furniture, pottery and prints are preserved) and a Library (hosting a rich collection of Franciscan manuscripts, many of which are illuminated).

# SAN FRANCESCO PICCOLINO
## (Infant St. Francis)

From the Chiesa Nuova a slightly descending lane leads to a narrow opening where below a flat arch lies the entrance of the Oratorio di San Francesco Piccolino.

The small church belongs to the Friars Minor and, according to eminent scholars, is the place where Madonna Pica gave birth to Francis. The restorations done during the past centuries dismantoled the house of Pietro di Bernardone.

The arch was added in 1281 by the nephew of the Saint, Piccardo, to give the site more dignity. On approaching the small ogival arch above the entrance, we notice the inscription making explicit reference to the nativity: "HOC ORATORIUM FUIT BOVIS ET ASINI STABULUM IN QUO NATUS SAN FRANCISCUS MUNDI SPECULUM". The translation is: "This Oratory was the stable of an ox and donkey, in which St. Francis, mirror of the world, was born".

*The Oratorio di San Francesco Piccolino (exterior).*

The interior, probably the draper's shop of Bernardone's house, was consecrated in the second half of the 13th century through the good offices of Piccardo. The rectangular and sober room shows the original bare stone. The pointed arch vault was decorated, as well as the walls, where there are traces of frescos of the 13th, 14th and 15th centuries.

More relevant findings are behind the altar and represent scenes from the Saint's life. The return to a simple style, according to the Franciscan ideals, was made possible after the restoration of 1926 when the stuccoes adorning the interior were removed. The ideal analogy of the Oratorio di San Francesco Piccolino with the stable of Bethlehem gives even greater mysticism to the place.

*The bare interior of San Francesco Piccolino.*

# CATTEDRALE DI SAN RUFINO
## (St. Rufino's Cathedral)

After the visit to the Chiesa Nuova the tourist is advised to return to the Piazza del Comune, to pass by the fountain and to reach the upper half of the square where Via San Rufino begins. The street ends in the homonymous square where the Cathedral rises.

The church of San Rufino is a remarkable construction not only for its architectonic style (it is considered the most important Romanesque religious building in Umbria), but also for the meaning it has come to assume in the history of the Franciscan movement.

The first constructions were built on this site during the Roman period, but in the 8th century a small basilica was erected to host the body of St. Rufino, the first Bishop of Assisi, martyred in 238 A.D. At the beginning of the 11th century the Bishop of Assisi, Ugone, wanted another church built on it and then transferred there the Bishop's seat. Finally, Clarissimo, another Bishop of Assisi, decided to erect a new big temple

*The Cattedrale di San Rufino and the bell tower.*

*The faade of San Rufino seen from the bottom upwards.*

to preserve the body of the Saint. It was here that St. Francis preached for the first time.

The façade is divided in three sections by two plaster strips that give slenderness to the structure. The lower section consists of square panels that enclose the three portals. The construction is a fine specimen of Romanesque style and other examples can be found in southern Umbria and in northern Abruzzo (in the surroundings of L'Aquila). The three portals are variously decorated: at the base of the larger door there are two lions (the one on the left is holding a man, the other a ram), the animals at the base of the side portals on the other hand, are griffins. The lunettes are decorated with floral patterns, clinging animals, Christian symbols, several mouldings (in the lunette of the larger portal, inside a roundel is an enthroned Christ, outside are the figure of St. Rufino and a Madonna suckling her Child; in the lunette of the left door two lions are drinking; in the lunette of the right door are two big birds). The middle section of the façade begins with a row of columns delimited by two stone wolves (one on each end). Above this decoration are three rose windows of unquestionable artistic value. The central one is supported by three telamones standing on animals and on its four sides are the symbols of the four Evangelists. The upper section of the façade is relatively insignificant. It as an ogival arch which was perhaps meant to contain a mosaic decoration.

The high bell tower, with a clock on the first register, has a rectangular base and the lower and middle parts were already part of the church of the 11th century. The belfry, recently restored, is noteworthy.

The Romanesque style of the façade was lost in the interior, radically changed by Galeazzo Alessi in 1571. The restoration gave the interior a typical late Renaissance structure. It is a church with nave and two aisles furnished with altars. Beyond the left entrance is a small door leading to a Roman cistern which served as a base for the bell tower. At the side of the main entrance are statues of St. Clare and St. Francis by Amalia and Giovanni Duprè; on the side of the right entrance is the font where Francis and Clare were baptized (it was brought here from its original location in the church of Santa Maria Maggiore). The Baroque **Cappella del Sacramento** (Holy Sacrament's Chapel) housing several 17th century paintings, is on the right aisle. Farther along is a side entrance with a fine portal and the **Museo Capitolare** (Chapter Museum) with numerous paintings, sculptures and church ornaments.

Returning to the interior of the church, along the nave one arrives to the main altar where the remains of St. Rufino, St. Vitale and San Rufino d'Arce are kept. The apse is adorned by a fine wooden choir. To the left of the apse is the **Cappella della Madonna del Pianto** (Chapel of Our Lady of Tears), with a reproduction of the statue which, according to tradition, was seen to be crying at the end of the 15th century.

Outside again, we can visit the crypt of the previous church with a charming small apse and with a nave and two aisles. A beautiful Roman sarcophagus from the 3rd century, in which the body of St. Rufino was buried, a well, 28 metres deep, and the remains of an interesting Carolingian cloister of the 11th century can be seen.

Before going down to the Church of Santa Chiara, it is possible to visit the area where the ancient **Anfiteatro Romano** used to be. Today, within its bounds, civil buildings have been erected.

*Main entrance of San Rufino, detail.*

# BASILICA DI SANTA CHIARA
## (Basilica of St. Clare)

From Piazza San Rufino, enter the narrow street on the left (facing the Cathedral), cross Via Galeazzo Alessi and go down along Via Sermei to the Piazza Santa Chiara where the homonymous church rises.

The temple was erected in 1257 and consecrated eight years later. It was built following the rules of the Italian Gothic style, but with the characteristic Franciscan sobriety preached by St. Francis and St. Clare. The façade is made up of alternating bands of white and pink stone. In the lower section, the portal with slender marble columns stands out against the simplicity of the wall. Two lions are set on the sides of the lunette. In the central section there is a fine rose window with several concentric circles and twisted columns. The building, designed by Brother Filippo da Campello, was reinforced by means of three flying buttresses to support the vault (14th century). The bell tower has a rectangular floor plan and ends in a spire. The irregular square in front of the Basilica has been completely repaved a couple of years ago. In the

*The fog snuggles up to the city.*

*The Basilica di Santa Chiara, exterior.*

middle of the square stands a nice polygonal fountain (1872). From the artificial terrace on which the square is located it is possible to admire a panoramic view of the northern Umbrian Valley.

The interior is plain and bare (with fragments of frescoes on the left of the entrance). It is a church with a single naves, in Gothic style, with cross vaults. The temple was built on a previous church dedicated to St. George, that housed St. Francis' body from his death to the transfer to the great Basilica.

About half way along the nave, beyond the entrance of the crypt, is the **Cappella del Crocifisso** (Chapel of the Crucifix), so named because it hosts the Crucifix which spoke to St. Francis at the beginning of his conversion. Opposite, beyond the grill, some relics of St. Clare and St. Francis are preserved. The next chapel is the **Cappella del Sacramento** (Chapel of the Holy Sacrament), with several interesting frescoes of Giotto's school, such as the *Descent from the Cross*, the *Deposition in the Sepulchre*, the *Resurrection*, *St. George and the Dragon*, the *Nativity*, the *Adoration of the Three Magi*. On the other side of the nave is the **Cappella di Santa Agnese** (St. Agnes' Chapel) where the remains

*The Crucifix which spoke to St. Francis in the Chiesa di San Damiano is kept in the Church of St. Clare.*

of some of Clare's nuns are kept.

The presbytery is partly frescoed by Maso di Stefano, who in the vaults reproduced several Saints. Above the altar is a Crucifix (13th century); on the left side of the transept, is a wooden painting with a Maestà, while in the right transept we find the beautiful *Tavola del Maestro di Santa Chiara* (Wooden painting of the Master of St. Clare), with the figure of the Saint surrounded by eight scenes from her life. The cycle has to be read from bottom left: *Clare meets the Bishop Guido, Clare being welcomed by Francis at the Porziuncola, Clare takes the habit, The Saint resisting her father, Agnes resisting her relatives who want to prevent her entering the convent, The cross appearing on the loaf of bread, The deathbed, Funeral of the Saint.*

The crypt was completed in 1872 to keep the remains of the Saint, found in 1850 in a sepulchre below the main altar.

Clare was born from a noble family of Assisi in 1194, in an environment that encouraged her spiritual inclinations. Her own dispotion and the example of Francis forged a soul that was already devoted to renunciation and solitary life. In 1212 Clare fled to the Porziuncola where Francis cut her hair and where she took the Franciscan habit devoting herself to a life of penitence. After a short stay at the Monastery of Benedectines of St. Paul in Bastia, where her father did everything in his power to take her back home, Clare established her residence at San Damiano and here founded the Order of the Poor Ladies, which changed it's name to Poor Nuns of St. Clare after the death of the Saint. She stayed at San Damiano forty-two years. In spite of her perpetual illness, she initiated many sisters to religious life, preached charity and poverty, comforted the suffering, received the visit of high prelates and Popes. In 1243 St Clare succeeded in driving the Saracens out of the convent. She consecrated her life to meditation and was a bright example of hope and unquestioned integrity. St. Clare died in 1253 and was canonized two years later by Pope Alexander IV

*St. Clare, detail of the wooden painting by the Maestro di Santa Chiara.*

*Santa Maria Maggiore, the ancient cathedral of the city.*

## SANTA MARIA MAGGIORE
### (Church of St. Mary Major)

From Piazza Santa Chiara, going along Via Sant'Agnese, we reach
Piazza del Vescovado (where the Bishop's Palace is located). On the
south side of the square is the **Chiesa di Santa Maria Maggiore**. It was
built on a Roman temple (several remains are in the crypt) and was the
first cathedral of Assisi before the construction of the church of San
Rufino. The façade is bare, the bell tower dates back to the 14th century.
The interior, with nave and two aisles, shows numerous fragments of
frescoes. Francis was baptized here.

## SAN FRANCESCUCCIO
### (Little St. Francis' Oratory)

Entering Via Antonio Cristofani (a historian of the city) from Piazza del
Vescovado, after two hundred metres on the left is the Oratorio di San
Leonardo (also called of San Francescuccio). On the outside wall there is
a fresco of the 15th century, entitled *The works of Mercy*.

## FONTE MARCELLA
### (Marcella Fountain)

Going down to Via Fontebella, the street offers a beautiful view of the
valley. The Fonte Marcella is on the right side of Via Fontebella. It is a
fountain with a rectangular basin, built in 1556.

*Fonte Marcella, detail.*

*An evocative image of the Chiesa di San Pietro.*

## CHIESA DI SAN PIETRO
**(St. Peter's Church)**

At the end of Via Fontebella is Piazzetta (small square) Ruggero Bonghi. Turning to the left towards Piaggia di Porta San Pietro, at the bottom is the very interesting church of San Pietro, which is the conclusion of the itinerary inside the city walls.

The church was built at the end of the 10th century and was restructured in the 13th century.

The rectangular façade is in Romanesque style. It is divided into two sections by a cornice formed by small hanging arches; the lower part is characterized by three portals, the impressive central one is decorated at the base by two stone lions. In the upper part there are three magnificent rose windows (the central one is the biggest).

The interior, with a nave and two aisles, is impressive and solemn. The huge pillars and the restoration made in 1954, which led to the removal of Baroque stuccoes, give the place a feeling of auterity. The presbytery is elevated by some steps above the nave. Several frescoes of the 14th century are noteworthy.

# SACRED PLACES IN THE SURROUNDINGS OF ASSISI

After having visited the city, it would be interesting to spend a couple of days in the sacred places nearby Assisi, fundamental to Franciscan history. We can start from the Monastery and the Church of San Damiano, the little Church of San Masseo, the Church of Rivotorto and then climb up Mount Subasio where the Eremo delle Carceri and the Abbey of San Benedetto are, which are both extremely evocative. It goes without saying that a visit to the Sanctuary of Santa Maria degli Angeli, with the Porziuncola, the cradle of the Franciscan movement, is not to be missed. If there is still some time left, you can organize an excursion to the fortified villages around Assisi, mostly situated in the north-west of the town.

## SAN DAMIANO
### (Church and Convent of San Damiano)

The church can be reached following the sign set in Viale Vittorio

*The entrance of the monastic complex of San Damiano.*

*The little church of San Damiano, interior.*

Emanuele II. Proceed along a winding and steep road until you get to an opening where it is easy to park, then take a short path up to a little square where the entrance of San Damiano lies.

At the beginning of his conversion, young Francis would frequently pause here. The crucifix hung on the wall of the crumbling construction said to him: "Francis, go and restore my house that is falling in ruins". Francis sold all his belongings, defied his father's anger and bought all that was necessary to repair the church. St. Clare lived here from 1211 until 1253 and St. Francis, tired and ill, rested here for some time and composed the Canticle of the Creatures, a poem of touching lyricism and spirituality. When he died, the funeral procession, before the body's burial in San Giorgio, stopped at San Damiano, where the Poor Clares were able to pay the Saint the last respect. In this place St. Clare performed several miracles: the multiplication of the loaves of bread and the oil, the sign of the cross on the bread, the Saracens' expulsion, some extraordinary healings and, finally, the vision of a service in the Basilica di San Francesco, which she was unable to attend.

The little church is dark, narrow, its walls blackened by candle smoke, nevertheless it emanates deep emotion; above the altar hangs a copy of the Crucifix which spoke to Francis (the original is kept in Santa Chiara). The little apse is embellished by a little wooden choir (16th century) and there is a fresco with the figures of Madonna with Child, St. Damian and St. Rufino (12th century).

On the right from the little choir is the entrance to the ancient Convento delle Clarisse (Poor Clares' Convent) with several rooms, among which the Coretto of Santa Chiara (Private Chapel of St. Clare), used as a place of prayer. A narrow staircase leads to the place where St. Clare used to grow flowers. Following the old convent, we reach the Oratory with frescoes, the Dormitory, where Blessed Clare died, the Cloister, immersed in perfect silence, the Refectory, with the original furnishings (the place where Blessed Clare used to sit is marked) and the Infirmary.

From here, **San Masseo** can be reached by foot, where there is a church built in Romanesque style in 1059. The crypt, with a nave and two aisles, is one of the oldest in Assisi.

*Façade of the little church of San Damian, detail. The flowers recall Clare who stayed here forty-two years.*

# SANTA MARIA DI RIVOTORTO
## (Church of St. Mary of Rivotorto)

Santa Maria di Rivotorto is a couple of kilometres away from San Damiano. The present building, in neo-Gothic style, dates back to 1854 and was built up on the ruins of a temple (16th century) that collapsed during an earthquake and it still has the function of preserving the **Sacro Tugurio** (Holy Hovel), where St. Francis and his first companions met used to meet and where he dictated the first Rule of the Order. Here the first Franciscan Community was officially founded.

The church, recently restored, has in the ogival arch of the upper part of the façade a decoration representing the *Fiery Chariot*, to the memory of Francis' apparition to his companions. The place was also witness of many other prodigious events. The Tugurio consists of three different parts joined together by a little central chapel; on the left was the kitchen, on the right a little dormitory.

*The Chiesa di Santa Maria di Rivotorto.*

*The Abbazia di San Benedetto, on the side of Mount Subasio.*

# ABBAZIA DI SAN BENEDETTO
**(Abbey of San Benedetto)**

Going up from Rivotorto to the northeastern side of Assisi, at a
biforcation leave Viale Vittorio Emanuele II and take Via Madonna
dell'Olivo and then go along Via San Benedetto which, after about two
kilometres, leads to the Abbey.

Its history has been troubled from the beginning; it was built in the 11th
century and partly destroyed in the second half of the 14th century.
Restored only in the 17th century, it had already lost its original
splendour. Recently a more accurate restoration brought to light the
boundary walls, the Romanesque crypt, the apse, some stone columns, a
second crypt with three columns. New researches and the discovery of
some important documents have proved that its origin dates back to the
7th century, at least.

# EREMO DELLE CARCERI
## (The Hermitage)

It can be reached from the Abbey of San Benedetto, going along the street that ascends Mount Subasio. An easier route starts from Piazza Matteotti (in the upper part of the city, following the signs).

Long ago the slopes of Mount Subasio were "sprinkled" with several hermitages, places of contemplation and silence in immediate contact with nature. Among these is the Eremo delle Carceri, a solitary spot, 790 metres above sea level, that always interested and attracted Francis. The Saint and his companions often came here to meditate and from 1206 to 1211 visited the place very frequently. Holm oaks and oaks frame the solitary site. The Monastery is a complex of buildings nestled over the Fosso (ravine) delle Carceri. The visit begins from a small cloister with

*The Eremo delle Carceri (Hermitage) situated on the green slopes of Mount Subasio.*

*The entrance to the Eremo delle Carceri (Hermitage).*

two wells and continues through the refectory, the friars' cells, the Chiesetta di San Bernardino (St. Bernardino's Chapel) with a remarkable 15th century choir, the Cappella di Santa Maria delle Carceri (Chapel of St. Mary), consecrated in 1216, St. Francis' cave (where he usually slept and meditated), the Oratory.

The path, that leads to the wood is very charming and impressive. Here is the secular holm oak where, according to tradition, birds listened to the Saint's words. In the wood there are the caves of his first companions: Rufino, Masseo, Antonio da Stroncone, Bernardo da Quintavalle, Andrea, Egidio and Silvestro. Coming back to the monastery the visit goes on with the Conventino di San Bernardino, the Coretto and the Cappellina della Maddalena.

*Eremo delle Carceri (Hermitage), detail.*

*The complex of the Hermitage seen from the wood.*

# MOUNT SUBASIO:
# NATURE AND LANDSCAPE

Mount Subasio, which is 1290 metres high, is a very important point of reference for the visitors of St. Francis' famous country.

It is situated between the Chiascio and Topino valleys and its elliptic shape rises like a solitary black. The upper area resembles a whale's back, a shape that is quite common in the hills of central italy.

The mount is essentially a calcareous formation and the geological structure reveals either the presence of solid limestone or of red and white scales.

Whereas the lower part of Subasio is characterized by sandstone formations, in the upper half considerable karstic phenomena are quite evident, such as dolines caused by the corrosion produced, in the limestone substructure, by meteorological agents. The doline of the Mortaro Grande, formed by the collapse of the superficial earth crust, is very famous. Noteworthy are also the six caves situated near Spello

The Subasio is full of springs, which find their origin in the impermeable substrates to be found both on the eastern and the western slopes of the mountain. One of the more important ones is the Santo Ruggio, which

*Perspective of Assisi from Mount Subasio.*

*A wild flower on Mount Subasio.*

lies very cluse to the town.

There are several ravines on the western and eastern sides of the mount, which become the beds of perennial or occasional streams, such as the Fosso delle Carceri which, according to a well-known tradition, fills with water only when catastrophe is imminent.

The landscape of the Subasio is characterized by three different horizontal zones of vegetation.

The lower area is the one that has been shaped most by human activity, and the olive trees covering this zone convey a pleasant silver grey hue to the cultivated land.

The central part of the Subasio, the richest in natural or artificially planted woods, is a line of demarcation between the inhabited lower part and the pastures and meadows of the higher area.

Both homogeneous and varied patches of wood are to be found. The most common species covering the area of the Fosso Renaro and growing on soils rich in minerals are hornbeams, mountain maples, bay oaks and ashes. The beech, a species typical for high mountains, is found in the upper woodland zone and on the northern slope of the mountain.

Most outstanding for its beauty and compactness is the grove of holm oaks that grows around the Eremo delle Carceri, near the homonymous precipice.

The sunlight scarcely penetrates the closely planted trees, thus giving rise to a disquieting dance of gloomy shadows.

The Corps of Foresters are carrying out experiments in reforestation on the Subasio, which lead to the implantation of species that do not belong to the region, such as cedars, black pines and cypresses.

To complete the description of the vegetation shrubby species and little trees like the hawthorn, the box, the juniper, laburnum and elder have to be mentioned.

In the upper part, above the woodland zone, there is just grassy vegetation, apart from some beech trees. Here wild pasturing led to a decay of the original flora.

The fauna of the Subasio consists of several mammals such as squirrels, beech-martens, loirs, dormice, foxes, mice and non-migratory birds.

The massive human presence and the uncontrolled hunting caused the diminution and, in same cases, the disappearance of species such as roe deers, grey and Greek partridges, wolves and royal eagles.

For people fond of trekking there are about thirty footpaths throughout Mount Subasio. Some of them have been marked by wooden signs and by white and red spots on rocks and on trees. Most of these footpaths are easy to walk even for people who are not used to mountain excursions. The others need more attention, better equipment and, above all, an adequate knowledge of the territory.

*Water is life.*

# THE FORTIFIED VILLAGES

Leaving the city in the direction of Perugia, along the old main road just after a kilometre, turn right to Petrignano. After about three kilometres on the left, you can ascend to a place called **Tordibetto**, which has an old medieval castle with round towers. Not far from here is the castle of **Beviglie** (15th century), according to the historians the birthplace of Brother Elia, a very important figure of the Franciscan Order. From here, **Mora**, with the ruins of an ancient castle, can be easily reached. The fortified village of **Sterpeto**, the oldest castle in Assisi, is well preserved. To get there, return to the main road and follow the sign to Sterpeto. Carlo Borromeo stayed there for a short time. **Rocca San'Angelo** is probably the most charming and interesting village nearby, for the presence of the **Chiesina di Santa Maria in Arce** dating back to 13th century, where several paintings, by artists such as Bartolomeo Caporali, Dono Doni, Matteo da Gualdo and Giovanni Spagna, are kept. **San Gregorio**, on the other hand, is the best preserved and the biggest among the fortified villages.

*The fortified village of San Gregorio.*

*Colour and tradition during the Calendimaggio.*

# FESTIVITIES AND FOLKLORE

Several festivities are organized by various associations all over Assisi (for a complete list, contact the tourist board in Piazza del Comune). Most of them have a religious nature and are connected with St. Francis, first of all the Feast of St. Francis (on October 3rd and 4th), the indulgence of Santa Maria (at the beginning of August), the Franciscan Studies Congress (in October), the celebrations of Holy Week (with the evocative Procession of the Dead Christ). The Antiques exhibition (held in Bastia Umbra) and the important National Literary Prize Insula Romana (founded and developed in Bastia) are two important cultural events.

But the best known festival in Assisi is the **Festa del Calendimaggio**.

The origin of the Calendimaggio looses itself in the mists of time. It probably has Roman origins. In May the Romans celebrated the coming of Spring, because it was considered to be of good omen. In the Middle Ages the religious meaning of the event was lost and the aspects involving challenge and fight among knights were more and more emphasized. What did remain in the spirit of the contenders was the symbol of spring as the season of renewal and the flowering of love, an unrepeatable moment of freedom and an occasion to forget wars and famines, and against the background of this medieval scenery with its high towers and mighty walls, people sought to redeem themselves from poverty and indigence. The feast of the Calendimaggio was an unrepeatable occasion to be free. During the first days of May, the streets and alleys of Assisi filled with music, dances and rhymes. The most beautiful girl of the city was elected "Spring's Queen" and was entitled to open the dances. Around the 14th century the city was divided in two factions: the *Parte de sopra* (Part from Above) and the *Parte de sotto* (Part from Below). Guelfs and Ghibellins (represented by the families of Nepis and Fiumi) fought bloody was in the attempt to conquer the supremacy over Assisi. During Calendimaggio, the division of Assisi in *Parte de sopra* and *Parte de sotto* is still alive but the original spirit of the festival, as a greeting to Spring and a love hymn, is now back. The election of Madonna Primavera is one of the most meaningful moments and, during this period, the streets are animated by musical contests, medieval processions, crossbowmen and displays of flags. Deep emotions arise when the torches shake in the wind and light up the hearts of people in costume and of the spectators.

*Participation and "ensigns" : two components of the festival.*

# SANTA MARIA DEGLI ANGELI

Turning the eyes towards the plain from any one of the balconies of Assisi, we cannot help seeing the urban and industrial area which clusters around the shape of a huge dome that tands out from a religious structure. We are talking about Santa Maria degli Angeli, the most populated hamlet of Assisi with its 7,000 inhabitants.

Its growth started in the latter half of the last century, when, as a result of the opening of the railroad tract between Rome and Florence the possibility of craftsmanship and industrial activity emerged, tourism increased and the urban area became more important (before then there were only a few old houses huddling around the church). The influx of pilgrims attracted to the place in occasion of the Indulgence of the Porziuncola (from 1216) was greatly increased after the construction of the Santuario. The Basilica was built in order to give protection to the Porziuncola (buiding works started in 1569).

Santa Maria degli Angeli does not haven many monuments, except for the **Palazzo dei Capitani del Perdono** (the palace hosting the magistrates in charge of the feast of the Pardon), with its elegant

*The dome of the Basilica di Santa Maria degli Angeli stands out from the plain.*

*Basilica Patriarcale di Santa Maria degli Angeli, detail.*

columned portico. It is located in the central Piazza Garibaldi, in front of the northern side of the church. The construction began in 1616. The interior is not very interesting. Another point not to be missed is the **Fontana delle "26 cannelle"** (Fountain of the Twenty-six Spouts). It was built for Cosimo de' Medici in the early part of the 15th century (it was originally situated where now we find the Palazzo dei Capitani del Perdono).

# LA BASILICA PATRIARCALE
# DI SANTA MARIA DEGLI ANGELI
## (The Patriarchal Basilica of Santa Maria degli Angeli)

Its huge dimensions (126 metres in length, 65 metres in width and 75 metres in height) make it one of the biggest religious buildings of Christianity.

The first stone was laid on March 25th, 1569 and the plan was by Galeazzo Alessi from Perugia, with the collaboration of Vignola and Danti. Work progressed less quickly than usually because all those Franciscan Friars who abhorred earthly pomp were highly contrary. Moreover, in order to build the church several important Franciscan remains, such as the Cappella delle Memorie, a great part of the monastery and a choir set behind the Porziuncola (built expressly by San Bernardino da Siena), had to be destroyed. Some of them were in very bad conditions, but undoubtedly they had a deep meaning for those Franciscan friars strictly following St. Francis' thought. The construction required a long period of time, but the façade was finished at the end of the 16th century, the interior in 1679, while the dome and the bell tower (in conformity with the original plan by Alessi) were completed the following year. In 1832 an earthquake of considerable intensity caused the façade to collapse, so it was rebuilt, but the present structure, with an added portico (following the project by Cesare Bazzani), is the result of

*The façade of the Basilica di Santa Maria degli Angeli.*

a new restoration carried out in the twenties of this century. In 1930 the statue of the Madonna (by Colasanti) was placed on top of the façade.

The bright and spacious interior is, by and large, rather simple; the linear patterns and the agile stuccoes make clear the function of preserving one of the most touching Franciscan remains and of giving shelter to the pilgrims coming to the Basilica for prayer. The church is with a nave and two aisles; there are several chapels where above the altars we find noteworthy frescoes. The painting by Federico Zuccari (1592), housed in the Cappella della Natività (the fifth of the right aisle), represents the theme of the Pardon.

*The Porziuncola inside the Basilica.*

# THE PORZIUNCOLA

The little church of the Porziuncola, one of the most touching symbols of the Franciscan religious feeling, is overhung by the big Basilica and its architectonic dimensions seem to be annihilated by the surrounding geometry of lines. It is one of the symbols, maybe the most important symbol of religiousness of this earth (and not only).

The meanings ascribed to this holy place are numerous: the cradle of the Franciscan movement, undisputed shrine of the Original Word, Francis' favourite refuge, point of reference for the irradiation of the message to the world. There are innumerable episodes in St. Francis' life linked to the Porziuncola, starting from 1208, when the Saint found his definitive path in the wood which at that time surrounded the construction. The chapel belonged to the Benedictines who had the intention to donate it to Francis, but he accepted only to rent it against payment of a basket of fish. So the Porziuncola became the centre of gravity for the Franciscan Movement all over the world. Here the first friars decided to leave in order to preach a new way of thinking and acting, here the journeys that led all over Europe and Africa with the aim of converting people to

*The polyptyc by Ilario da Viterbo is on the back wall of the Porziuncola.*

poverty and renunciation were organized and here the news of the first martyrdoms arrived. Several miraculous episodes are connected to this place. When Francis, for instance, in order to avoid the Devil, threw himself into a thorn bush and the blood flowing from the wounds changed the bush into a rose garden. God wanted to recompense Francis for having resisted the devil's temptation and He consented to forgive all those who repented and entered the Porziuncola, and in 1216 Pope Honorius III authorized the Indulgence.

The original structure, the walls and the apse of the small building have not undergone any changes. The wooden portal dates back to the 15th century; the neo-Gothic shrine was added later. The fresco covering the upper part of the façade represents the Indulgence of the Pardon and was made by Federico Overbek in 1830. The outer walls and the little apse show some traces of frescoes. The interior, darkened by the passage of time, is original and very evocative. On the altar wall the most valuable painting of the church stands out. It is a polyptyc painted in 1393 by Ilario da Viterbo. The main scene is about the request and the granting of the Pardon. Francis, surrounded by a crowd of angels, lifts up a rose crown to Christ and Our Lady. In the lower big panel the Annunciation is portrayed, with the Archangel bending down in front of the Virgin Mary in meditation; the vase of lilies in the background is a symbol of purity. Several other episodes concerning the Pardon are arranged around these two main scenes: Francis throwing himself into the thorn bush to send away the devil; the angels who will take him before God. The figures of ten saints make up the frame. They are, from the right, Leonardo, Giacomo, Caterina martyr, Blessed Angela da Foligno, Benedetto, Francis, Clare, Agnes, Rufino and Anthony Abate.

*Inside the Cappella del Transito St. Francis died.*

## CAPPELLA DEL TRANSITO

At the time of Francis, near the Porziuncola there was a little infirmary. A small door leads inside. Here St. Francis abandoned his tired body in the evening of October 3rd, 1226. Later, the little building was called Cappella del Transito, as a memory of that event.

Above the door, on the outside wall, there is a fresco by Domenico Bruschi (1886) representing St. Francis' death: Francis is lying on the rough brick floor, surrounded by his distressed companions and by an angels' choir. On the side wall is another fresco about the funeral of the Saint. In the interior, Giovanni Spagna portrayed Francis' closest companions and above the little altar is a terra-cotta statue of the St. Francis (15th century) by Andrea della Robbia.

*The polyptyc in enamelled terra-cotta by Andrea della Robbia.*

*The Crucifix by Giunta Pisano (Museum of the Sanctuary).* ➤

# THE CRYPT AND THE APSE

Recent excavations made beneath the altar to construct a crypt led to the discovery of some traces of Franciscan buildings. Inside the crypt, behind the altar, is a wonderful work by Andrea della Robbia. It is a glazed terra-cotta polyptyc with several scenes: The crowning of the Virgin, The receiving of Stigmata, the Annunciation, the Nativity and the Adoration of the Magi.

The semicircular apse, which has recently been lifted up together with a part of the presbytery in order to consent the construction of the underlying crypt preserves a nice wooden choir of the end of the 16th century.

The furnishings and the delightful ceiling of the Sacrestia (Sacristy) are worth visiting.

# THE ROSE GARDEN

A sign leads the visitor to the Rose Garden where even now the roses bloom without thorns. The place recalls the episode when Francis threw himself into the thorn bush to avoid the devil and his blood changed the thorns into odorous flowers.

*The monument to Francis with a sheep.*

*Roses in the Rose Garden of Santa Maria degli Angeli.*

# THE CAPPELLA DELLE ROSE
**(Rose Garden Chapel)**

Near the Rose Garden is the **Cappella delle Rose**, the place where St. Francis used to rest. Here one can see the Saint's Grotto, where some tree trunks seemingly dating back to Francis' times have been placed.

The Cappella delle Rose was completely frescoed by Tiberio d'Assisi in the 16th century and recently restored: the paintings represent several episodes of St. Francis' life such as those concerning the first followers' and those about the Indulgence of the Porziuncola.

The route, suggested by the friars themselves, leads to the Cappella del Pianto, to a moving Crib, to an antique chemist's and finally to the **Museo del Santuario**, full of documents, sacred objects, sculptures, furniture, wooden altar pieces. The image of *St. Francis* by Cimabue, the other one by the Maestro di San Francesco and, above all, the *Crucifix* by Giunta Pisano (1236) are not to be missed.

We should not forget to visit the **Vecchio Convento**, with San Bernardino and the other friars' cells and the impressive room of the "common fire". The Library of the Sanctuary and the Museo di Arte e Artigianato del Terzo Mondo (Third World Art and Cafts Museum) are points of interest, too. (This latter is in a building that is about 200 metres away from the basilica).

## THE CANTICLE OF THE CREATURES

*Most high omnipotent good Lord, to Thee praise, glory, honour, and every benediction.*

*To Thee alone Most High do they belong. And no man is worthy to pronounce Thy Name.*

*Praise be to Thee my Lord with all Thy creatures. Especially for Master Brother Sun who illuminates the day for us, and Thee Most High he manifests.*

*Praise be to Thee my Lord for Sister Moon and for the stars, in Heaven Thou hast formed them, shining, precious, fair.*

*Praise be to Thee my Lord for Brother Wind, for air and clouds, clear sky and all the weathers through which Thou sustainest all Thy Creatures.*

*Praise be to Thee my Lord for Sister Water, she is useful and humble, precious and pure.*

*Praise be to Thee my Lord for Brother Fire, through him our night Thou dost enlighten, and he is fair and merry, boisterous and strong.*

*Praise be to Thee my Lord for our Sister Mother Earth, who nourishes and sustains us all, bringing forth divers fruits and many coloured flowers and herbs.*

*Praise be to Thee my Lord for those who pardon grant for love of Thee and bear infirmity and tribulation, Blessed be those who live in peace, for by Thee Most High they shall be crowned.*

*Praise be to Thee my Lord for our Sister Bodily Death from whom no living man can flee; woe to them who die in mortal sin but blessed they who shall be found in Thy most holy Will; to them the second death can do no harm.*

*O bless and praise my Lord all creatures, and thank and serve Him in deep humility.*

*St. Francis*

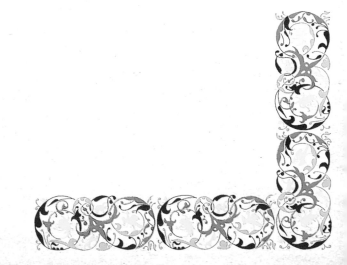

## A SIMPLE PRAYER

O Lord make of me an instrument of Thy peace;
Where there is hatred, let me put love,
Where there is resentment let me put forgiveness,
Where there is discord let me put unity,
Where there is doubt let me put faith,
Where there is error let me put truth
Where there is despair let me bring happiness.
Where there sadness let me bring joy,
Where there is darkness let me bring light.
O Master grant that I may desire rather:
To console than to be consoled.
To understand rather than to be understood.
To love rather than to be loved.
Because it is in giving that we receive;
In forgiving that we obtain forgiveness;
In dying that we rise to eternal life.

*Franciscan sources*

# USEFUL ADDRESSES

TOURIST INFORMATION OFFICES:
Piazza del Comune, 12      ☎ 075 8138680

INFORMATION AND HOTEL RESERVATION OFFICE
Largo Properzio (Porta Nuova)      ☎ 075 816766

INFORMATION AND HOTEL RESERVATION OFFICE
(Assisan Association of Hotel Keepers)
S.S. 147 Assisana      ☎ 075 816566
     ☎ 075 813599

**REGIONAL AIRPORT - S. Egidio**      ☎ 075 594141

## EMERGENCY CALLS:

POLICE EMERGENCY      ☎ 113
CARABINIERI EMERGENCY CALLS      ☎ 112
FIRE STATION EMERGENCY CALLS      ☎ 115
A.C.I. ROAD SERVICE      ☎ 116
DIVISIONAL POLICE STATION - Assisi      ☎ 075 819091
CARABINIERI - Assisi      ☎ 075 8190800
CARABINIERI - Petrignano      ☎ 075 8038021
CARABINIERI - Santa Maria degli Angeli      ☎ 075 8040210
LOCAL TRAFFIC WARDENS - Assisi      ☎ 075 812820
FIRST AID AMBULANCE CALLS      ☎ 118

## TAXIS

PIAZZA SAN FRANCESCO - Assisi      ☎ 075 812606
PIAZZA SANTA CHIARA - Assisi      ☎ 075 812278
PIAZZA DEL COMUNE - Assisi      ☎ 075 813193
PIAZZA UNITÀ D'ITALIA - Assisi      ☎ 075 812378
STAZIONE FERROVIARIA - S. Maria degli Angeli      ☎ 075 8040275
PIAZZA GARIBALDI - S. Maria degli Angeli      ☎ 075 8041605
RADIO TAXI - Assisi      ☎ 075 813100

COMUNE DI ASSISI
Piazza del Comune - 06081 Assisi (PG)      ☎ 075 81381

# TRAVEL NOTES

# TRAVEL NOTES

# TRAVEL NOTES

# TRAVEL NOTES

# CONTENTS

# FRANCIS GOES ON LIVING AND ACTING THROUGH THE CENTURIES BY MEANS OF THE LIVELY FAMILY
## EVOLUTION OF THE ORDER OF FRIARS MINOR AND ITS BRANCHING OUT FROM THE FOUNDATION TILL TODAY

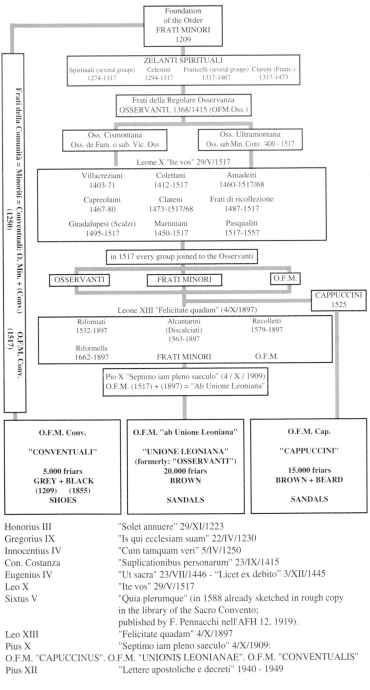

Foundation
of the Order
FRATI MINORI
1209

ZELANTI SPIRITUALI

| Spirituali (several groups) 1274-1317 | Celestini 1294-1317 | Fraticelli (several groups) 1317-1467 | Clareni (Fratic.) 1317-1473 |

Frati della Regolare Osservanza
OSSERVANTI, 1368/1415 (OFM Oss.)

Oss. Cismontana
Oss. de Fam. o sub. Vic. Oss

Oss. Ultramontana
Oss. sub Min. Conv. '400 - 1517

Leone X "Ite vos" 29/V/1517

| Villacreziani 1403-71 | Colettani 1412-1517 | Amadeiti 1460-1517/68 |
| Capreolanti 1467-80 | Clareni 1473-1517/68 | Frati di ricollezione 1487-1517 |
| Guadalupesi (Scalzi) 1495-1517 | Martiniani 1450-1517 | Pasqualiti 1517-1557 |

in 1517 every group joined to the Osservanti

OSSERVANTI    FRATI MINORI    O.F.M.

CAPPUCCINI
1525

Leone XIII "Felicitate quadam" (4/X/1897)

| Riformati 1532-1897 | Alcantarini (Discalciati) 1563-1897 | Recolletti 1579-1897 |
| Riformella 1662-1897 | FRATI MINORI | O.F.M. |

Pio X "Septimo iam pleno saeculo" (4 / X / 1909)
O.F.M. (1517) + (1897) = "Ab Unione Leoniana"

Frati della Comunità = Minoriti = Conventuali: O. Min. + (Conv.)
(1250)

Conventuali: O. Min. + (Conv.) (1517)

O.F.M. Conv.

**O.F.M. Conv.**

"CONVENTUALI"

5.000 friars
GREY + BLACK
(1209)    (1855)
SHOES

**O.F.M. "ab Unione Leoniana"**

"UNIONE LEONIANA"
(formerly: "OSSERVANTI")
20.000 friars
BROWN

SANDALS

**O.F.M. Cap.**

"CAPPUCCINI"

15.000 friars
BROWN + BEARD

SANDALS

| Honorius III | "Solet annuere" 29/XI/1223 |
| Gregorius IX | "Is qui ecclesiam suam" 22/IV/1230 |
| Innocentius IV | "Cum tamquam veri" 5/IV/1250 |
| Con. Costanza | "Suplicationibus personarum" 23/IX/1415 |
| Eugenius IV | "Ut sacra" 23/VII/1446 - "Licet ex debito" 3/XII/1445 |
| Leo X | "Ite vos" 29/V/1517 |
| Sixtus V | "Quia plerumque" (in 1588 already sketched in rough copy in the library of the Sacro Convento; published by F. Pennacchi nell'AFH 12, 1919). |
| Leo XIII | "Felicitate quadam" 4/X/1897 |
| Pius X | "Septimo iam pleno saeculo" 4/X/1909: |
| O.F.M. "CAPUCCINUS". O.F.M. "UNIONIS LEONIANAE". O.F.M. "CONVENTUALIS" |
| Pius XII | "Lettere apostoliche e decreti" 1940 - 1949 |